First World War
and Army of Occupation
War Diary
France, Belgium and Germany

1 INDIAN CAVALRY DIVISION
Lucknow Cavalry Brigade
'G' Ammunition Column Royal Horse Artillery
31 August 1914 - 27 March 1915

WO95/1175/2

The Naval & Military Press Ltd
www.nmarchive.com
Published in association with The National Archives

Published by

The Naval & Military Press Ltd

Unit 10 Ridgewood Industrial Park,

Uckfield, East Sussex,

TN22 5QE England

Tel: +44 (0) 1825 749494

www.naval-military-press.com

www.nmarchive.com

This diary has been reprinted in facsimile from the original. Any imperfections are inevitably reproduced and the quality may fall short of modern type and cartographic standards.

© Crown Copyright
Images reproduced by permission of The National Archives, London, England, 2015.

Contents

Document type	Place/Title	Date From	Date To
Heading	WO95/1175/2		
Heading	B.E.F. 1 Ind Cav Div Lucknow Bde. "G" Ammo Col RHA 1914 Aug to 1915 Mar		
Heading	War Diary of "G" Ammunition Column R.H.A. From 31-18-14 to 30/10/14 Volume I		
War Diary	Lucknow	31/08/1914	31/10/1914
War Diary	Port Said.	01/11/1914	30/11/1914
Heading	War Diary of "G" Ammunition Column R.H.A. From 1-12.14. to 31-12.14 Volume I		
War Diary	Orleans	01/12/1914	24/12/1914
War Diary	Lieres.	24/12/1914	25/12/1914
War Diary	St Hilaire	25/12/1914	30/12/1914
Heading	War Diary of "G". Ammunition Column. 1st Indian Cavalry Division From 1st January 1915 To, 31st January 1915		
War Diary	St Hilaire	01/01/1915	31/01/1915
War Diary	Cottes (St. Hilaire)	18/01/1915	31/01/1915
Heading	War Diary of "G" Ammunition Column R.H.A. 1st Indian Cavalry Division From 1st February 1915 to 28th February 1915		
War Diary	Inclusive	02/02/1915	11/02/1915
War Diary		12/02/1915	12/02/1915
War Diary		13/02/1915	26/02/1915
War Diary		01/02/1915	02/02/1915
War Diary		01/02/1915	28/02/1915
Heading	War Diary of "G" Ammunition Column, R.H.A 1st Indian Cavalry Division From 3rd March 1915 27th March 1915		
War Diary		03/03/1915	27/03/1915

WO95/11175/2

B.E.F

1 Ind Cav Div

Lucknow Bde.

"G" Ammo Col RHA

1914 Aug – 1915 Mar

War Diary of
"C" Ammunition Column R.H.A.

From 31-8-14
To. 30/11/4

Volume I
Pp. 1. to 9.

Page 1.

Army Form C. 2118.

WAR DIARY
or
INTELLIGENCE SUMMARY.

(Erase heading not required.)

September 1914
"D" Amn. Column. R.H.A

Instructions regarding War Diaries and Intelligence Summaries are contained in F.S. Regs., Part II, and the Staff Manual respectively. Title pages will be prepared in manuscript.

No 3 Section
A. G's Office at Base
I.E. Force
Passed to Genl S. Sectn
on 8. 12-14

Hour, Date, Place.	Summary of Events and Information.	Remarks and references to Appendices
Lucknow. Aug 31. 1914. 10 a.m	Orders received to mobilize. New strength of R.H.A. Section to be as follows:- British. 1 Subaltern. 1 B.Q.M.S. 1 Sergt. 1 Bombadier. 8 Gunners. 1 Farrier. 1 Shoeing Smith. 1 Saddler. Indian. 1 Havildar Driver. 1 Naick Dr. 22 Drivers. 1 Shoeing Smith. 1 Havildar Gunner. 1 Naick Gunner. 16 Gunners. Followers. 1 Mochi. 1 Laugri. 1 Mehtar. Horses. 19 Riding. (including two for C.O) } 61. 44 Draught 1st Reinforcement. 1 Havildar. 5 Ranks. All deficiencies to be made up from "D" Amn. Column at Ahmednagar. Transport and personnel for S.A.A. section to be supplied later	Horses and men surplus to new establishment almost entirely absorbed by "U" Battery. R.H.A.
Sept. 14th 1914	Mobilization completed.	

Page 2.

Army Form C. 2118.

WAR DIARY
or
INTELLIGENCE SUMMARY.
(Erase heading not required.)

Instructions regarding War Diaries and Intelligence Summaries are contained in F. S. Regs., Part II, and the Staff Manual respectively. Title pages will be prepared in manuscript.

October 1914.

G. Ammunition Column. R.H.A.

Hour, Date, Place.		Summary of Events and Information.	Remarks and references to Appendices
October 8th 1914.	6 a.m	Unit entrained and left for Bombay.	
October 10th 1914.	7 a.m	Troop train arrived at Bombay. Orders were received to embark as follows :—	
		A. H.T. "Velturia". Lt with McCormel. 20 Indian Ranks. 56 horses.	
		B. H.T. "Itria" 14 British Ranks. 5 horses. 6 Amn. Wagons. 1. G.S. wagon 276 rounds of 13 pr. Q.F. Amn.	
		C. H.T. "Laomedon". 12 Indian Ranks.	
		D. H.T. "Franz Ferdinand" 17 Indian Ranks. 3 followers.	
	6 p.m	Embarkation of "A" Completed	
	7 p.m	" " B. Completed.	Temperature very high.
October 11th.		"Velturia" & "Itria" proceeded out into stream and anchored. C. & D. embarked. Arrangements were with difficulty made for the B.Q.M.S. and Farrier to form party A. The former performed duties of Ships Q.M.S. throughout voyage	
Oct. 16th	5 p.m	Entire Convoy started.	
Oct. 24th	7.30 a.m	Convoy were abreast of Aden. Did not stop.	These six days at anchor in harbour were very trying for the horses who suffered severely.
Oct. 30th	4 a.m	Arrived at Suez and anchored.	The fact that the unit was divided up on four ships entailed much extra work for all concerned & considerable difficulty over forage & returns
Oct. 31st.	2 p.m	Arrived at Port Said and anchored	

Page 3.

Army Form C. 2118.

WAR DIARY
or
INTELLIGENCE SUMMARY.

(Erase heading not required.)

November. 1914.   G. Ammunition Column. R.H.A.

Instructions regarding War Diaries and Intelligence Summaries are contained in F.S. Regs., Part II, and the Staff Manual respectively. Title pages will be prepared in manuscript.

Hour, Date, Place.	Summary of Events and Information.	Remarks and references to Appendices
Nov. 1st. 1914. Port Said.	Left anchorage & passed outside to anchor again. Took on much fresh bran and barley before leaving.	Rations given to horses on voyage as follows :—
Nov. 7th. 7 am	Passed Malta.	Oct 16th–25th. Bran. 7 lbs. Oats. 3. Barley 2.
Nov. 10th. 1 am	Reached Marseilles. Came alongside quay at daylight.	" 26th " 5 " 3 " 3.
Nov. 11th	Disembarked party from Nevasa, and collected men, horses, & vehicles from "Itria" and "Laomedon". All ranks issued with home pattern clothing. Changed pistol ammunition issued in India. Drew 8 rifles and pouch ammunition for same.	" 27th " 5 " 2 " 3.
		" 28th–31st " 4 " 2 " 4.
		Nov. 1st–3rd " 3 " 2 " 5.
		" 4th–10th " 5 " Gram 2. " 3.
12 noon	Left by march route for La Valentine Camp. (10 miles) St Carrol and Oscar Barany joined for duty as interpreters.	During voyage Nos 26 and 35 Batteries suffered from fever and lymphangitis. Otherwise no sickness of any sort among horses of this unit. They were all on upper decks.
Nov. 19th. 12 noon	Left by march route to entrain. At station received 17 men and 3 followers from "Franz Ferdinand". Despatched 1 Havildar and 5 men to Indian Military Base Depot at Parc Borley.	Forage in camp La Valentine. Bran. 3. Barley 2. Oats. 3. Gram 3. = 12 lbs
7 pm	Left by train. "C" Ammunition Column also in train. The Armourer Staff Sergeant of 1st K.D.Gs joined for duty with unit.	
Nov. 22nd. 12.30 am	Arrived at Orleans, and proceeded to Les Grues Camp.	Forage at Orleans. Bran. 2. Barley 3. Oats. 4. Gram. 3.
Nov. 25th.	1 Indian officer and 8 ranks joined for duty with S.A.A section from 36th Cavalry.	During this period, obtained 24 carts for gun ammunition from 31st Mule Cart Coys.
Nov. 30th.	Left by train. C Ammunition Column still at Orleans.	29 for S.A.A from Bharatpur mule Corps. The latter in good state. Former different. Many articles of equipment & clothing now of poor stamp. Harness I have reported to be unserviceable.

Arthur Oswell
Capt. R.H.A.

"War Diary
of
"G" Ammunition Column R.H.A.

From 1- 12. 14.
To 31- 12. 14.

Volume II

Page 40
Army Form C. 2118.

"G" Ammunition Column. R.H.A.

WAR DIARY
or
INTELLIGENCE SUMMARY.
(Erase heading not required.)

Instructions regarding War Diaries and Intelligence Summaries are contained in F. S. Regs., Part II, and the Staff Manual respectively. Title pages will be prepared in manuscript.

Hour, Date, Place.		Summary of Events and Information.	Remarks and references to Appendices
Dec. 1. 1914. ORLEANS		Still in camp.	W.H.McC
Dec. 7. 1914	5.30 pm	Started to entrain unit.	
	8.35 pm	Train left.	
Dec. 9 1914	3.30 a.m	Arrived at BERQUETTE. Detrained in 4 hours and proceeded by march route to billets at AUCHEL.	W.H.McC
		The three columns "B" "C" "G" are now formed into 1 Divisional Amn Column belonging to 1st Ind Cav. Div, and is divided into "B" "C" "G" Sections.	No Head Quarter Staff for unit yet provided. This is desirable, as it takes 1 officer away from his work and 1 QMS / clerk have much extra work in collecting reports from the other two Sections.
		Four heavy horses, 1 G.S. wagon, 2 A.S.C. drivers and 1 Indian Driver joined unit at railhead.	
		The strength of this unit (G) now is.	
		2 B.Os. 2 I.Os. 17 Europeans. 51 Indian Ranks. 58 Mule drivers. 5 followers	
		32 Riding horses. 48 draught horses. 106 mules. 6 Amn waggons. 53 mule carts. 2 G.S. waggons. 1 water cart. Also 1 B.O and 1 French Interpreter.	
Dec. 14. 1914.		Received orders to be ready to move at an hour's notice.	W.H.McC
Dec. 20 1914	2.45 p.m.	"C" Section detached to join up with AMBALA Brigade near BETHUNE. Interpreter O. Barany left. He was unsuitable for his work.	W.H.McC
Dec. 21 1914.	2.30 a.m	The S.A.A. Section of "B" left to join the SIALKOTE Brigade, near BETHUNE.	W.H.McC
Dec. 22. 1914	10 am	Orders received at 5.30 am to move to new billets at once. Counter order arrived when we were ready. Finally left at 10 am for HERES. Interpreter E. Braun joined as vice O. Barany.	As Q battery R.H.A. were not required, the rest part of B. did not move.
Dec. 23.	7.30 pm	The S.A.A. Section of B rejoined unit.	W.H.McC
Dec. 24.	3 pm	"C" Section rejoined unit	

Army Form C. 2118.

WAR DIARY
or
INTELLIGENCE SUMMARY.

(Erase heading not required.)

G. Ammunition Column. R.H.A.

Instructions regarding War Diaries and Intelligence Summaries are contained in F.S. Regs., Part II, and the Staff Manual respectively. Title pages will be prepared in manuscript.

Hour, Date, Place.		Summary of Events and Information.	Remarks and references to Appendices
Dec. 24.	LIERES.	4:30 p.m. Orders received to be ready to move at moment's notice. 8 p.m. Above order cancelled. Billets for night.	M.H.McC
Dec. 25.		10:30 a.m. Marched to ST HILAIRE - COTTES to new billets. "B" and "G" in COTTES.	M.H.McC
Dec. 25th – 31st.	ST HILAIRE.	ST HILAIRE, "C" in COTTES. In billets. During this period, orders received from 1st. I.C.D. H.Qrs to proceed with systematic training, but to be ready to move at four hours notice. Also that sanction has been given for the Divisional Ammunition Column to be re-organized as laid down in War Establishments. Expeditionary Force. 1914.	M.H.McC
Dec. 30th.		Jemadar Abdul Samad, 36th Jacobs Horse, returned to his regiment, Unsuitable. Jemadar Yar Mahomed arrived.	M.H.McC

Notes during December 1914.

Health of Europeans. Excellent.
" " R.M.A. Indians. Excellent. } Not a single case of sickness of any sort.

" " Transport Corps Drivers. During the month, five were admitted to hospital. The men are of a very poor stamp physically, and, in my opinion, the wastage from sickness when they have to undergo exposure will be very great. No men to replace them are at present available. Consequently R.M.A. Indian gunners have to take their place, and the efficiency of the unit, as a whole, is greatly impaired.

" " Horses. } Good. A few cases of colds with slight temperature have occurred.
" " Mules. }

M.H. McConnel Capt R.H.A.

WAR DIARY
OF
"G" Ammunition Column, 1st Indian Cavalry Division.

From 1st January 1915 To, 31st January 1915

Army Form C. 2118.

WAR DIARY

INTELLIGENCE SUMMARY.

(Erase heading not required.)

"G" Ammunition Column.
1st Ind. Cav. Division

Instructions regarding War Diaries and Intelligence Summaries are contained in F. S. Regs., Part II, and the Staff Manual respectively. Title pages will be prepared in manuscript.

Hour, Date, Place.	Summary of Events and Information.	Remarks and references to Appendices
Jan. 1. 1915. ST HILAIRE	Still in Billets.	
Jan. 10. 1915.	One BEGBIE Signaling lamp allowed per column.	Suggest that in future, Lamps for Signaling purposes be issued to R.H. and R.F.A. At present they are not authorized nor are the new tested in their use at annual inspection.
Jan. 18. 1915.	Parade for whole Cavalry Corps. Sir John French inspected many units, but did not come to Divisional troops of 1st Ind. Cav. Division. B.Q.M.S. Kingston, on promotion to 2nd Lieutenant, left unit and proceeded to base	
Jan. 19. 1915.	Lieut. I. D Guthrie, 17th Cavalry, in charge of Small arm Section left to join Hd. Qrs. Royal Flying Corps on probation. Divisional Exercise.	
Jan. 22. 1915.	Lieut Shortridge, attached 29th Deccan horse, joined unit for duty. Vice Guthrie	
Jan. 23. 1915.	Six horses from Column left to join "U" Battery. R.H.A.	
Jan. 26. 1915.	Six remounts arrived to replace horses sent to "U" Battery. Good horses	
Jan. 29. 1915.	"A" "Q" "U" Batteries and "B" "C" "G" Columns less S.A.A. Sections left by march route to join 28th Division. 5th Corps 2nd Army. Billeted at STEENBECQUE for night (10 miles).	
Jan. 30. 1915.	Continued march, and billeted at BORRE (8 miles).	
Jan. 31. 1915.	Major Watson Colonel Kishen Singh accompanied this unit, as practically all A.T. carts in all 3 Columns belong to BHARATPUR Transport Corps. Halts of R.H.A. Section good. A.T. Cart drivers go sick easily.	During this march, 3 rations for Indian Ranks were a difficulty. Being an entirely English division, this was bound to happen to begin with. Serious difficulties arise owing to there being no Spare men, mules, or harness allowed for the 24 A.T. carts carrying boxed 13 pr Ammunition. M.H. McCraith Capt. R.H.A. O. nd g. G Ammunition Column.

Army Form C. 2118.

WAR DIARY of B. Amm. Col Reppt
for month of January 1915

INTELLIGENCE SUMMARY.

(Erase heading not required.)

Instructions regarding War Diaries and Intelligence Summaries are contained in F. S. Regs., Part II, and the Staff Manual respectively. Title pages will be prepared in manuscript.

Hour, Date, Place.	Summary of Events and Information.	Remarks and references to Appendices
30 Jan 1915	Left ST HILAIRE with RHA Section to join the XXVIII Div. of 5th Army Corps. Convoys taking up the line near YPRES (the 27th & 28th Divs, with RHA Section of Amm Col OP, 1st Indian Cav Div, marched factory on that day) Arrived STEEN BECKE — billeted close for the night	Stw
31st Jan 1915	Left STEEN BECKE. Arrived BORRE when the Div. A. C. went into West NCU. From Jan 1 to Jan 30 the Div. Amm Col remained billeted at ST HILAIRE. On the departure of the 3 RHA Sections on the 30th the S.A.A. Section was left behind at ST HILAIRE. 5 days leave was granted to Officers, and known on return from each section of the Column during January	Stw

[signature] Capt RFA
Off'g OC 'B' Section W. Div Am. Col.

Army Form C. 2118.

WAR DIARY
or
INTELLIGENCE SUMMARY.
(Erase heading not required.)

"C" Ammunition Column
R1/14

Instructions regarding War Diaries and Intelligence Summaries are contained in F. S. Regs., Part II, and the Staff Manual respectively. Title pages will be prepared in manuscript.

Hour, Date, Place.	Summary of Events and Information.	Remarks and references to Appendices.
COTTES (ST HILAIRE)		
18th Jan 1915	Capt H.S Maydwell 30th Lancers admitted to Hospital	1st to 30th Jan The column remained in billets, Route marches, different training & concerts given
28th Jan. 1915	Capt H.T Walker. 30th Lancers joined	
	6 horses transferred to "U" Bty. R.H.A.	
30th Jan. 1915. 12 noon.	Artillery Section left billets marched to STEENBECQUE via AIRE	30th Jan A, Q & U Batteries RHA & Div Am Col RH ordered to proceed to the neighbourhood of YPRES & join the 28th Div. 5th Army Cols given
	S.A Section remained in billets. 6 remounts joined	
31st Jan. 1915	Artillery Section marched to BORRE via HAZEBROUCK	

Serial No 91.

WAR DIARY

"G" Ammunition Column; R.H.A, 1st Indian Cavalry Division.

From 1st February 1915 to 28th February 1915

Army Form C. 2118.

WAR DIARY
or
INTELLIGENCE SUMMARY.

(Erase heading not required.)

G. Ammunition Column. R.H.A.
1st Ind. Cav. Div.

Instructions regarding War Diaries and Intelligence Summaries are contained in F. S. Regs., Part II, and the Staff Manual respectively. Title pages will be prepared in manuscript.

Hour, Date, Place.	Summary of Events and Information.	Remarks and references to Appendices
Feb. 1. 1915	Two Sections of "A", one of "Q" and "U" Batteries, accompanied by 4 wagons of "C", two each of "B" and "G" Columns under Capt. J.L.C. White proceeded ahead. Remainder of Columns remained in billets at BORRE.	M.H.C.
Feb. 2. 1915. 6.50 a.m.	Proceeded by march route to billets about 1½ miles S of VLAMERTINGHE, and 3 miles from YPRES. "U" Battery billets ½ mile away. Battery in action about 2 miles E of YPRES. The 3. R.H.A. Batteries of 1st. Ind. Cav. Div. here form a brigade, and the 3. R.H.A. Sections of the Ammunition Column form a brigade ammunition Column under Lt. Col. H. Rouse. R.H.A.	M.H.C. M.H.C.
Feb. 2-11th. inclusive.	Remained in same billet supplying ammunition as required. During this period Saddler Brigham returned from hospital. Horses stood the exposure very well.	M.H.C.
Feb. 12th. 10 a.m.	Left by march route to billets about ½ mile N. of ABEELE. (12 miles) via VLAMERTINGHE and POPERINGHE. Arrived at 3.15 pm.	M.H.C.
Feb. 13th. 7.30 a.m.	Left by march route to old billets at ST HILAIRE (29 miles) via STEENVOORDE - HAZEBROUCK - AIRE. Mules did very well especially as there was heavy rain and wind in their faces. Arrived at 4.20 pm. Seven mule drivers (14. M.T.C.) arrived as a reinforcement.	M.H.C.
Feb. 14th.	Lt. G.C. Shakerley (29th Lancers) rejoined unit. Capt. H.S. Stewart (17th Cavalry) joined this unit to take over S.A.A. Section.	M.H.C.
Feb. 28th.	Condition and health of men and animals excellent during this month. M.H.Cornwall. Capt. R.H.A. Cmdg. Brvid. Amm. Col.	M.H.C.

Army Form C. 2118.

WAR DIARY
or
INTELLIGENCE SUMMARY.
(Erase heading not required.)

"C" Ammunition Column. R.H.A

Instructions regarding War Diaries and Intelligence Summaries are contained in F. S. Regs., Part II, and the Staff Manual respectively. Title pages will be prepared in manuscript.

Hour, Date, Place.	Summary of Events and Information.	Remarks and references to Appendices.
Feb. 1st 1915	Marched from BORRE to VLAMERTINGHE & billeted in a farm 1½ m S.E. VLAMERTINGHE.	see
Feb. 2nd – 12th 1915.	"A", "Q" & "U" batteries in action near YPRES. "A" battery wagon-line, 300 yds from position of ammunition column. Refilling point ½ S. of VLAMERTINGHE on VLAMERTINGHE – OUDERDOM road. Replenishment of ammunition carried out from wagon lines at night. The Belgian Artillery took over from "A" & "U" batteries on the nights 10th-11th, 11th-12th.	see
Feb. 12th 1915.	Marched from VLAMERTINGHE to ABEELE & billeted for night.	see
Feb. 13th 1915.	Marched to ST-HILAIRE. COTTES & went into same original billets, which the column left on 30th Jan.	
Feb. 13th – 28th 1915	Remained in billets. Lieut. C. I. McKay R.H.A. joined 19/2/15.	see

Gulab Singh & Sons, Calcutta—No. 22 Army C.—5-8-14—1,07,000.

WAR DIARY

"G" Ammunition Column, R.H.A. 1st Indian Cavalry Division.

From 3rd March 1915 to 31st March 1915

WAR DIARY

INTELLIGENCE SUMMARY.

(Erase heading not required.)

Army Form C. 2118.

g Ammunition Column RHA
1st Indian Cavalry Division.

Instructions regarding War Diaries and Intelligence Summaries are contained in F. S. Regs., Part II, and the Staff Manual respectively. Title pages will be prepared in manuscript.

Hour, Date, Place.	Summary of Events and Information.	Remarks and references to Appendices
March 3rd 1915	Received orders as follows:- Amn Column A.J Carts & baggage together will trigger g"R', 'Q' + 'V' Batteries + RA Head Quarters to move to rendezvous at Rly Crossing W of MERVILLE leaving starting point BOUREQAT 6 p.m. Ammunition Wagons marching in rear of 'A', 'Q' + 'V' Batteries to leave starting point at 9.0 a.m 4/3/15 & proceed to the same rendezvous. Both Columns to wait at rendezvous till 6 am 4/3/15 for the billeting party. The A.J Carts under Captain Wilson RHA left billets at 5.30pm & arrived at rendezvous distance 14 miles at 1 a.m 4-3-15. Batteries & Ammunition wagons left at 1.30 am 4/3/15. The Small Arm Section of the Divisional Column remained in billets at St HILAIRE. So much SAA having been retained 2 days before to the Service Park, there were now 8 empty A.T Carts, of these, it sent up with the RHA Section to spare carts. The remaining 4 being left as spare with the S.A. Section.	

Army Form C. 2118.

WAR DIARY
INTELLIGENCE SUMMARY.
(Erase heading not required.)

Hour, Date, Place.	Summary of Events and Information.	Remarks and references to Appendices
March 4 - 1915	Went into billets in farm 2 miles N of MERVILLE at VIERHOUCK. Capt M.W. McConnel RHA, having been posted to 11th Brigade RHA Ammunition Column, left the unit. Lieut M. J. Motzay joined the Column in temporary command of B Section. 'W' Battery RHA went into action S of LAVENTIE with firing battery & first line wagons, but all horses were left in billets at MERVILLE. The Ammunition supply by the Column is direct to the Battery position, and at night. The Refilling point in about 2 miles S of VIERHOUCK at TISSAGE.	
March 5 - 1915	Supplied ammunition at night to 'W' Battery RHA in action.	
March 7 - 1915 4pm	Received orders at 4pm to move to new billets on MERVILLE - HAVERSKERQUE road. Left VIERHOUCK at 5.30pm. Were much delayed on the road 2 miles W of MERVILLE by meeting a brigade of Infantry with their transport & the Column did not get into billets until 1.0am 8/3/15. Whilst marching an order was received for 10 wagons of ammunition to be	

Army Form C. 2118.

WAR DIARY
or
INTELLIGENCE SUMMARY.
(Erase heading not required.)

Instructions regarding War Diaries and Intelligence Summaries are contained in F.S. Regs., Part II, and the Staff Manual respectively. Title pages will be prepared in manuscript.

Hour, Date, Place.	Summary of Events and Information.	Remarks and references to Appendices
March 9th - 1915	Supplied to the Battery position. 'G' Column supplied his wagons.	
	Received orders to move next day as follows:- Ammunition Column to move up & billet at LA BRIANNE 1 mile E. of Neuville & with the exception of the ammunition wagons which were to proceed to Battery RUE DE PARADIS near R.A. Head Quarters, this being only about 1 mile from the three batteries 'A', 'O' & 'J'.	
March 10th - 1915 8 am	Left billets & arrived at new billets at LA BRIANNE at 10 am. Capt White at 10 am took all the horses of 'A','O' & 'V' batteries (the battery Captains having gone up to the Battery position) to RUE DE PARADIS.	
	Capt Wilson R.H.A. left at 12 noon with the ammunition wagons of the Column to the Same place.	
	The battery horses & Column were placed in adjacent fields N of RUE DE PARADIS.	
	A.T. Carts & G.S. Wagons remained at LA BRIANNE under Lieut McKAY R.H.A.	
March 11th - 1915	To lessen the distance between LA BRIANNE & the RUE DE PARADIS - 8 miles, a replenishing point was established in the Farm Yard in ESTAIRES only 3 miles from the RUE DE PARADIS. To this place 30 A.T. Carts	

Army Form C. 2118.

WAR DIARY
INTELLIGENCE SUMMARY.
(Erase heading not required.)

Instructions regarding War Diaries and Intelligence Summaries are contained in F.S. Regs., Part II, and the Staff Manual respectively. Title pages will be prepared in manuscript.

Hour, Date, Place.	Summary of Events and Information.	Remarks and references to Appendices
March 13th 1915	Under D.M.S. Sves remained permanently being replaced by full men when enlisted.	
	As a few shrapnel fell over replenishing point in ESTAIRES, this was moved back 1 mile to a field in the western outskirts of ESTAIRES (the fighting at or near Neuve Chapelle, which commenced at 7.30 a.m. on 10/3/15 was now over).	
March 18th 1915	Ammunition wagons/personnel at Rue de PARADIS + AT Carls de ESTAIRES returned to LA BRIMINE.	
March 24th 1915	Received information that British personnel to replace Indian, in reorganisation of the 3 Sections "B" C+G with one Divisional Amm. Column in the British Expeditionary Force Establishment had arrived at Anchy au Bois.	
March 27th 1915	"G" Ammunition Column R.H.A ceased to exist as a separate unit, cross went on the arrival of part of the British personnel.	

Field
31-3-15

Vaughn Capt RHA
Comdg G. Amm Col
RHA

www.ingramcontent.com/pod-product-compliance
Lightning Source LLC
Chambersburg PA
CBHW081251170426
43191CB00037B/2121